pasta sauces

simple and delicious easy-to-make recipes

Christine McFadden

p

This is a Parragon Publishing Book
This edition published in 2003

Parragon Publishing
Queen Street House
4 Queen Street
Bath, BA1 1HE, UK

Copyright © Parragon 2002

ISBN: 1-40542-025-1

Printed in China

Produced by the Bridgewater Book Company Ltd.

Photographer Simon Punter

Home Economist Ricky Turner

Cover by 20 Twenty Design

NOTES FOR THE READER

- This book uses both imperial and metric measurements. Follow the same units of measurement throughout; do not mix imperial and metric.

- All spoon measurements are level: teaspoons are assumed to be 5 ml, and tablespoons are assumed to be 15 ml.

- Unless otherwise stated, milk is assumed to be whole milk, eggs and individual vegetables such as carrots are medium, and pepper is freshly ground black pepper.

- Recipes using raw eggs should be avoided by infants, the elderly, pregnant women, convalescents, and anyone suffering from an illness.

- The times given are an approximate guide only. Preparation times differ according to the techniques used by different people and the cooking times may also vary from those given. Optional ingredients, variations, or serving suggestions have not been included in the calculations.

contents

introduction

Cooked in minutes and easy on the purse, pasta is one of the most versatile of foods, combining happily with a wide variety of sauces. Although meat-based sauces are among the best known, vegetables provide inspiration for many delicious sauces, as do fish and seafood.

Pasta comes in a large number of shapes: flat and round ribbons, tubes, quills, and corkscrews, to name but a few. Each shape lends itself to a particular sauce style. For example, long, thin pasta, such as spaghetti, is best for tomato or oil-based sauces. The sauce coats the surface and clings to it as you twirl the pasta round a fork. Wide, flat ribbons, such as fettucine, go well with cream sauces. Shapes or short, hollow tubes are perfect for chunkier sauces because they trap tasty morsels in their crevices.

To cook perfect pasta, use a large pan so the pasta has enough room to move around freely. Allow 4 cups of water for every cup of dried pasta (4 oz/115 g). Bring the water to a fast boil, then add the salt and pasta together, stirring once. Cooking time depends on the type of pasta. It is ready when al dente—tender, but still firm to the bite and slightly chewy. Be careful not to overcook. It is better to cook the sauce before the pasta; sauces can be kept waiting, but pasta cannot—it becomes sticky!

guide to recipe key		
	easy	Recipes are graded as follows: 1 pea = easy; 2 peas = very easy; 3 peas = extremely easy.
	serves 4	Recipes generally serve four people. Simply halve the ingredients to serve two, taking care not to mix imperial and metric measurements.
	10 minutes	Preparation time.
	10 minutes	Cooking time.

creamy chicken & shiitake sauce,
page 20

raw tomato sauce with olive oil,
garlic & basil, page 48

spaghetti with anchovies, olives, capers
& tomatoes, page 70

mussels with tomatoes,
peppers & olives, page 88

meat & poultry sauces

Rich, hearty, meat-based sauces include the
universally popular spaghetti bolognese,
which needs no introduction. There are also
irresistible sauces made with coarse-cut
sausages or bacon and enriched with
tomatoes, mushrooms, or bell peppers.
Less well-known are more delicate sauces
made with chicken. These often include
generous amounts of cream and freshly
grated cheese for richness and flavor.
All the sauces are simple to prepare
and are equally suitable for relaxed
entertaining or family suppers.

classic bolognese
meat sauce

very easy	
serves 6 as an appetizer, 4 as a main course	
15 minutes	
1 hour, 15 minutes	

ingredients

2 tbsp olive oil	2 tbsp tomato paste
1 tbsp butter	½ cup dry white wine
1 small onion, chopped finely	salt and pepper
1 carrot, chopped finely	½ tsp freshly grated nutmeg
1 celery stalk, chopped finely	1¼ cups chicken bouillon
1 cup mushrooms, diced	½ cup heavy cream
2 cups ground beef	1 lb/450 g dried spaghetti
¼ cup unsmoked bacon or ham, diced	2 tbsp chopped fresh parsley, to garnish
2 chicken livers, chopped	freshly grated Parmesan, to serve

Heat the oil and butter in a large pan over a medium heat. Add the onion, carrot, celery, and mushrooms to the pan, then cook until soft. Add the beef and bacon to the pan and cook until the beef is evenly browned.

Stir in the chicken livers and tomato paste and cook for 2–3 minutes. Pour in the wine and season with salt, pepper, and the nutmeg. Add the bouillon. Bring to a boil, then cover and simmer gently over a low heat for 1 hour. Stir in the cream and simmer, uncovered, until reduced.

Cook the pasta in plenty of boiling salted water until al dente. Drain and transfer to a warm serving dish.

Pour half the sauce over the pasta. Toss well to mix. Spoon the remaining sauce over the top.

Garnish with the parsley and serve with Parmesan cheese.

macaroni with sausage, pepperoncini & olives

		ingredients	
very easy		1 tbsp olive oil	2 tsp dried oregano
		1 large onion, chopped finely	½ cup chicken bouillon or red wine
serves 6 as an appetizer, 4 as a main course		2 garlic cloves, chopped very finely	salt and pepper
		2 cups pork sausage, peeled and chopped coarsely	4 cups dried macaroni
			12–15 black olives, pitted and cut into fourths
10–15 minutes		3 canned pepperoncini, or other hot red peppers, drained and sliced	⅔ cup freshly grated cheese, such as Gruyère
		14 oz/400 g canned chopped tomatoes	
15 minutes			

Heat the oil in a large skillet over a medium heat. Add the onion and cook for 5 minutes until soft. Add the garlic and cook for a few seconds, until just beginning to color. Add the sausage and cook until evenly browned.

Stir in the pepperoncini, tomatoes, oregano, and bouillon. Season with salt and pepper. Bring to a boil, then simmer over a medium heat for 10 minutes, stirring occasionally.

Cook the macaroni in plenty of boiling salted water until al dente. Drain and transfer to a warm serving dish.

Add the olives and half the cheese to the sauce, then stir until the cheese has melted.

Pour the sauce over the pasta. Toss well to mix. Sprinkle with the remaining cheese and serve at once.

meat sauce with mushrooms & tomatoes

		ingredients	
very easy		3 tbsp olive oil	4 tbsp tomato paste
		4 cups ground beef	2 tsp dried oregano
serves 6 as an appetizer, 4 as a main course		4 cups mushrooms, sliced thinly	salt and pepper
		4 scallions, sliced thinly	½ cup bouillon or water
		4 garlic cloves, chopped very finely	4 cups dried conchiglie or gnocchi
10–15 minutes		14 oz/400 g canned chopped tomatoes	freshly grated Parmesan, to serve
40 minutes			

Heat 1 tablespoon of the oil in a large skillet over a medium heat. Add the beef and cook until lightly browned. Remove from the skillet and set aside.

Add the rest of the oil to the skillet and cook the mushrooms until softened. Stir in the onions and garlic, then cook for 2 minutes.

Tip the meat back into the skillet and stir in the tomatoes, tomato paste, oregano, salt, pepper, and bouillon. Bring the mixture to a boil, then reduce the heat and simmer over a medium–low heat for 30 minutes.

Cook the pasta in plenty of boiling salted water until al dente. Drain and transfer to a warm serving dish.

Pour the sauce over the pasta and toss well to mix. Serve with freshly grated Parmesan.

sausage & beef sauce with bell peppers & tomatoes

		ingredients	

	very easy	2 tbsp olive oil
		4 bacon rashers, chopped
		1 onion, chopped finely
		1 green bell pepper, seeded and
		  chopped finely
		1 cup mushrooms, sliced thinly
		4 garlic cloves, sliced thinly
		2 cups ground beef
		1 cup coarse pork sausage, peeled
		  and chopped
			1 lb 12 oz/800 g canned
			  chopped tomatoes
			1 fresh bay leaf
			6 tbsp tomato paste
			4 tbsp red wine or bouillon
			salt and pepper
			1 lb/450 g/4 cups dried penne or rigatoni
			6 fresh basil leaves, shredded
			
			freshly grated Parmesan, to serve

	serves 6 as an appetizer, 4 as a main course		
	15–20 minutes		
	1 hour 15 minutes		

Heat the oil in a large skillet over a medium heat. Add the bacon and cook until lightly browned. Add the onion, green bell pepper, mushrooms and garlic. Gently cook for 5–7 minutes until soft.

Stir in the beef and sausage, then cook until browned. Add the tomatoes and bay leaf. Bring to a boil, then simmer over a medium–low heat for 1 hour. Stir in the tomato paste and wine. Season with salt and pepper. Simmer for a few minutes more.

Cook the pasta in plenty of boiling salted water until al dente. Drain and transfer to a warm serving dish.

Pour the sauce over the pasta and toss well to mix. Sprinkle with the basil and serve with Parmesan.

chicken & onion
cream sauce

very easy	
serves 4	
10 minutes	
35 minutes	

ingredients

1 tbsp olive oil
2 tbsp butter
1 garlic clove, chopped very finely
4 boneless, skinless chicken breasts
salt and pepper
1 onion, chopped finely
1 chicken bouillon cube, crumbled
½ cup water
1¼ cups heavy cream

¾ cup milk
6 scallions, green part included,
    sliced diagonally
scant ⅓ cup freshly grated Parmesan
1 lb/450 g dried fettuccine

chopped fresh flatleaf parsley,
    to garnish

Heat the oil and butter with the garlic in a large skillet over
a medium–low heat. Cook the garlic until just beginning to color.
Add the chicken breasts and raise the heat to medium. Cook for
4–5 minutes on each side, or until the juices are no longer pink.
Season with salt and pepper. Remove from the heat. Remove
the chicken breasts, leaving the oil in the skillet. Slice the breasts
diagonally into thin strips and set aside.

Reheat the oil in the skillet. Add the onion and gently cook for
5 minutes, or until soft. Add the crumbled bouillon cube and the
water. Bring to a boil, then simmer over a medium–low heat for
10 minutes. Stir in the cream, milk, scallions and Parmesan.
Simmer until heated through and slightly thickened.

Cook the fettucine in boiling salted water until al dente. Drain and
transfer to a warm serving dish. Layer the chicken slices over the
pasta. Pour on the sauce, then garnish with parsley and serve.

cannelloni with chicken, ricotta & herbs

		ingredients	
🖌	easy	MARINADE	1 tsp freshly ground black pepper
		½ cup white wine vinegar	¼ tsp freshly grated nutmeg
🍴	serves 4	1 garlic clove, crushed	½ cup freshly grated Parmesan
		1 cup olive oil	2 cups ricotta cheese
			1 egg, lightly beaten
🥄	15–20 minutes + 30 minutes to marinate	2 tbsp olive oil	1 tbsp chopped fresh oregano
		4 boneless, skinless chicken breasts, diced	2 tbsp chopped fresh basil
		6 tbsp butter	8 oz/225 g dried cannelloni
🕐	1 hour	generous 2 cups heavy cream	⅔ cup freshly grated mozzarella
		1 tsp salt	

In a bowl, combine the vinegar, garlic, and olive oil for the marinade. Add the chicken and marinate for 30 minutes.

Heat 2 tablespoons of olive oil in a skillet. Drain the chicken and cook 5–7 minutes, stirring, until no longer pink. Set aside.

Melt the butter in a pan over a medium–high heat. Add the cream, salt, pepper, and nutmeg. Stir until thickened. Reduce the heat, then add the Parmesan and stir until melted. Remove from the heat.

Heat the oven to 350°F/180°C. In a large bowl, mix together the ricotta, egg, and herbs. Stir in the chicken. Stuff the cannelloni with the chicken mixture. Pour half the sauce into a 9 x 13 inch/23 x 33 cm baking dish. Place the stuffed cannelloni on top. Pour over the remaining sauce. Sprinkle with the mozzarella and cover with aluminum foil. Bake for 45 minutes. Let the dish stand for 10 minutes before serving.

creamy chicken
& shiitake sauce

		ingredients	
very easy	1⅓ cups dried shiitake mushrooms	generous 1 cup chicken bouillon
	1½ cups hot water	1¼ cups whipping cream
serves 4	1 tbsp olive oil	salt and pepper
	6 bacon strips, chopped	1 lb/450 g dried tagliatelle
	3 boneless, skinless chicken breasts,	½ cup freshly grated Parmesan
10 minutes + 30 minutes to soak mushrooms	sliced into strips	
	2 cups fresh shiitake	chopped fresh flatleaf parsley,
	mushrooms, sliced	to garnish
	1 small onion, chopped finely	
35 minutes	1 tsp fresh oregano or marjoram,	
	chopped finely	

Put the dried mushrooms in a bowl with the hot water. Let soak for 30 minutes, or until softened. Remove, squeezing excess water back into the bowl. Strain the liquid in a fine-meshed strainer and reserve. Slice the soaked mushrooms, discarding the stems.

Heat the oil in a large skillet over a medium heat. Add the bacon and chicken, then stir-fry for about 3 minutes. Add the dried and fresh mushrooms, the onion, and oregano. Stir-fry for 5–7 minutes, or until soft. Pour in the bouillon and the mushroom liquid. Bring to a boil, stirring. Simmer for about 10 minutes, continuing to stir, until reduced. Add the cream and simmer for 5 minutes, stirring, until beginning to thicken. Season with salt and pepper. Remove the skillet from the heat and set aside.

Cook the pasta until al dente. Drain and transfer to a serving dish. Pour the sauce over the pasta. Add half the Parmesan and mix. Sprinkle with parsley and serve with the remaining Parmesan.

farfalle with chicken, broccoli & roasted red bell peppers

		ingredients	
	very easy	4 tbsp olive oil	1 lb/450 g small broccoli florets
		5 tbsp butter	2⅔ cups dried farfalle or fusilli
	serves 4	3 garlic cloves, chopped very finely	6 oz/175 g bottled roasted red bell
		1 lb/450 g boneless, skinless chicken	peppers, drained and diced
		breasts, diced	generous 1 cup chicken bouillon
	15 minutes	¼ tsp dried chili flakes	
		salt and pepper	freshly grated Parmesan, to serve
	15 minutes		

Bring a large pan of salted water to a boil. Meanwhile, heat the olive oil, butter, and garlic in a large skillet over a medium–low heat. Cook the garlic until just beginning to color.

Add the diced chicken, then raise the heat to medium and stir-fry for 4–5 minutes, or until the chicken is no longer pink. Add the chili flakes and season with salt and pepper. Remove from the heat.

Plunge the broccoli into the boiling water and cook for 2 minutes, or until tender-crisp. Remove with a perforated spoon and set aside. Bring the water back to a boil. Add the pasta and cook until al dente. Drain and add to the chicken mixture in the pan. Add the broccoli and roasted bell peppers. Pour in the bouillon. Simmer briskly over a medium–high heat, stirring frequently, until most of the liquid has been absorbed.

Sprinkle with the Parmesan and serve.

chicken with basil
& pine nut pesto

		ingredients	
very easy		PESTO	2 tbsp freshly grated romano
		1⅔ cups shredded fresh basil	2 tbsp vegetable oil
		125 ml/4 fl oz extra-virgin olive oil	4 boneless, skinless chicken breasts
serves 4		3 tbsp pine nuts	12 oz/350 g dried fettuccine
		3 garlic cloves, crushed	freshly ground pepper
		salt	
10 minutes		½ cup freshly grated Parmesan	sprig of fresh basil, to garnish
15 minutes			

To make the pesto, put the basil, olive oil, pine nuts, garlic, and a generous pinch of salt in a food processor or blender. Purée the ingredients until smooth. Scrape the mixture into a bowl and stir in the cheeses.

Heat the vegetable oil in a skillet over a medium heat. Cook the chicken breasts, turning once, for 8–10 minutes, or until the juices are no longer pink. Cut into small cubes.

Cook the pasta in plenty of boiling salted water until al dente. Drain and transfer to a warm serving dish. Add the chicken and pesto, then season with pepper. Toss well to mix.

Garnish with a sprig of basil and serve warm.

noodles with chicken satay sauce

very easy	
serves 4	
10 minutes	
20 minutes	

ingredients

2 tbsp vegetable oil
1 lb/450 g boneless, skinless
   chicken breasts, cubed
1 red bell pepper, seeded and sliced
4 scallions, green part included,
   sliced diagonally
pinch of salt

8 oz/225 g dried vermicelli
   or spaghettini
generous ½ cup smooth peanut butter
1 tsp grated fresh ginger root
2 tbsp soy sauce
½ cup chicken bouillon

Heat the oil in a large skillet over a medium heat. Add the chicken and cook for 5–7 minutes until no longer pink. Add the bell pepper and scallions. Cook for 3 minutes, or until just soft. Remove from the heat.

Cook the pasta in plenty of boiling salted water until al dente. Drain and return to the pan.

Put the peanut butter, ginger, soy sauce, and chicken bouillon in a large pan. Simmer over a medium–low heat, stirring, until bubbling. Add the cooked vegetables, chicken, and pasta to the peanut mixture. Toss gently until coated with the sauce.

Transfer to a warm serving dish and serve immediately.

fusilli with bacon, eggs & mushrooms

		ingredients	
	very easy	1 tbsp olive oil	2 eggs, beaten
		4 strips lean bacon or pancetta	115 g/4 oz mozzarella, cubed
	serves 6 as an appetizer, 4 as a main course	2 cups mushrooms, sliced	
		2 cups fusilli or conchiglie	chopped fresh flatleaf parsley,
		salt and pepper	to garnish
	10 minutes		
	15 minutes		

Heat the oil in a skillet over a medium heat. Add the bacon and cook until crisp. Remove with tongs, leaving the drippings in the skillet. Cut into small pieces and keep warm.

Cook the mushrooms in the bacon drippings for 5–7 minutes, or until soft. Remove from the heat.

Cook the pasta in plenty of boiling salted water until al dente. Drain and return to the skillet.

Stir the mushrooms, beaten eggs, and the cheese cubes into the pasta. Season with pepper and toss until the eggs have coated the pasta and the cheese has melted.

Transfer to a warm serving dish. Sprinkle with the bacon pieces and parsley and serve at once.

rigatoni with spicy bacon & tomato sauce

very easy	
serves 4	
10 minutes	
45 minutes	

ingredients

6 tbsp olive oil	½ tsp dried chili flakes
3 garlic cloves, sliced thinly	salt and pepper
scant ⅓ cup lean bacon, chopped	4 cups rigatoni
1 lb 12 oz/800 g canned	10 fresh basil leaves, shredded
chopped tomatoes	2 tbsp freshly grated romano

Heat the oil and garlic in a large skillet over a medium–low heat. Cook until the garlic is just beginning to color. Add the bacon and cook until browned.

Stir in the tomatoes and chili flakes. Season with a little salt and pepper. Bring to a boil, then simmer over a medium–low heat for 30–40 minutes, or until the oil separates from the tomatoes.

Cook the pasta in plenty of boiling salted water until al dente. Drain and transfer to a warm serving dish.

Pour the sauce over the pasta. Add the basil and romano, then toss well to mix. Serve at once.

ham, tomato & chile sauce

		ingredients	
very easy		1 tbsp olive oil	1 lb 12 oz/800 g canned
		2 tbsp butter	chopped tomatoes
serves 4		1 onion, chopped finely	salt and pepper
		scant ⅔ cup ham, diced	4 cups bucatini or penne
		2 garlic cloves, chopped very finely	2 tbsp chopped fresh
10–15 minutes		1 fresh red chile, seeded and	flatleaf parsley
		chopped finely	6 tbsp freshly grated Parmesan
1 hour			

Put the olive oil and 1 tablespoon of the butter in a large skillet over a medium–low heat. Add the onion and cook for 10 minutes, or until soft and golden. Add the ham and cook for 5 minutes, or until lightly browned. Stir in the garlic, chile and tomatoes. Season with a little salt and pepper. Bring to a boil, then simmer over a medium–low heat for 30–40 minutes, or until thickened.

Cook the pasta in plenty of boiling salted water until al dente. Drain and transfer to a warm serving dish.

Pour the sauce over the pasta. Add the parsley, Parmesan, and the remaining butter. Toss well to mix. Serve immediately.

spaghetti alla carbonara

		ingredients	
very easy		2 tbsp olive oil	scant ¼ cup freshly grated romano
		1 tbsp butter	1 tbsp chopped fresh
serves 4		⅔ cup lean, smoked bacon, sliced	flatleaf parsley
		into thin strips	4 tbsp light cream
		3 eggs, lightly beaten	pepper
10–15 minutes		¼ cup freshly grated Parmesan	1 lb/450 g dried spaghetti
15 minutes			

Heat the oil and butter in a skillet over a medium–high heat. Add the bacon and cook for 4–5 minutes, or until browned. Remove from the heat. Combine the eggs, cheeses, parsley, and cream in a bowl, mixing well. Season with pepper.

Cook the pasta in plenty of boiling salted water until al dente. Drain and return to the skillet.

Quickly add the egg mixture to the pasta, tossing rapidly so that the egg cooks in the heat. Transfer to a warm serving dish.

Briefly reheat the bacon over a high heat. Add to the pasta, then toss again and serve at once.

vegetable sauces

With their flamboyant colors and fresh flavors, Mediterranean-style vegetables and herbs are perfect for pasta sauces. These are among the quickest and easiest sauces to prepare, ranging from the simple concoctions of chopped raw tomatoes, olive oil, and basil to more complex mixtures of roasted bell peppers and garlic, or asparagus and Gorgonzola. Pantry ingredients are put to good use: jars of artichokes, bell peppers, sun-dried tomatoes, and olives all contribute robust flavors that will please vegetarians and meat-eaters alike.

sun-dried tomato & goat cheese sauce

		ingredients	
very easy		1 tbsp butter	salt and pepper
		2 garlic cloves, sliced thinly	4 cups dried penne
serves 4		8 oz/225 g goat cheese, crumbled	
		1¼ cups milk	TO SERVE
		½ cup heavy cream	scant ⅓ cup freshly grated Parmesan
10 minutes		20 oil-cured sun-dried tomato halves	10 fresh basil leaves, shredded
		(in oil), chopped coarsely	
10–15 minutes			

Heat the butter and garlic in a skillet over a medium–low heat. Cook until the garlic is just beginning to color. Add the cheese and milk. Stir until the cheese has melted and formed a thick sauce.

Add the cream and sun-dried tomatoes. Cook for about 5 minutes, stirring frequently, until reduced by one-third. Season with salt and pepper. Remove from the heat.

Cook the pasta in plenty of boiling salted water until al dente. Transfer to a warm serving dish.

Briefly reheat the sauce over low heat. Pour over the pasta. Add the Parmesan and basil, then toss well to mix. Serve immediately.

sun-dried tomato
sauce with herbs

		ingredients	
very easy		3 oz/85 g sun-dried tomatoes (not in oil)	2 tsp chopped fresh oregano
			1 tsp chopped fresh rosemary
serves 4		3 cups boiling water	salt and pepper
		2 tbsp olive oil	3 cups dried fusilli
		1 onion, chopped finely	
10–15 minutes		2 large garlic cloves, sliced finely	TO SERVE
		2 tbsp chopped fresh flatleaf parsley	10 fresh basil leaves, shredded
			3 tbsp freshly grated Parmesan
20–25 minutes			

Put the tomatoes and boiling water in a bowl and let stand for 5 minutes. Using a perforated spoon, remove one-third of the tomatoes from the bowl. Cut into bite-size pieces. Put the remaining tomatoes and water into a blender and purée.

Heat the oil in a large skillet over a medium heat. Add the onion and gently cook for 5 minutes, or until soft. Add the garlic and cook until just beginning to color. Add the puréed tomato and the reserved tomato pieces to the skillet. Bring to a boil, then simmer over a medium–low heat for 10 minutes. Stir in the herbs and season with salt and pepper. Simmer for 1 minute, then remove from the heat.

Cook the pasta in plenty of boiling salted water until al dente. Drain and transfer to a warm serving dish. Briefly reheat the sauce. Pour over the pasta, then add the basil and toss well to mix. Sprinkle with the Parmesan and serve immediately.

tomato-chile sauce
with avocado & cilantro

		ingredients	
	very easy	3 tbsp olive oil	7 oz/200 g canned chopped tomatoes
		4 scallions, green part	salt and pepper
	serves 4	included, sliced finely	3 cups dried farfalle or conchiglie
		1 fresh green chile, seeded and	2 small avocados, peeled and cubed
		chopped very finely	juice of ½ lime
	15 minutes	2 garlic cloves, chopped very finely	6 tbsp chopped fresh cilantro
	20 minutes		

Heat 1 tablespoon of the oil in a skillet over a medium–low heat. Add the scallions and chile, then cook, stirring constantly, for 3–4 minutes, or until just soft. Add the garlic and cook until just beginning to color.

Stir in the tomatoes. Bring to a boil, then simmer the sauce over a medium heat for 10 minutes, stirring, until thickened. Season with salt and pepper.

Cook the pasta in plenty of boiling salted water until al dente. Drain and transfer to a warm serving dish.

Pour the sauce over the pasta. Add the avocados, lime juice, cilantro and remaining olive oil. Toss well to mix. Serve warm or at room temperature.

bell pepper & goat cheese sauce

		ingredients	
very easy		2 tbsp olive oil	salt and pepper
		1 tbsp butter	4 cups dried rigatoni or penne
serves 4		1 small onion, chopped finely	4½ oz/125 g goat cheese, crumbled
		4 bell peppers, yellow and red, seeded	15 fresh basil leaves, shredded
		and cut into ¾ inch/2 cm squares	10 black olives, pitted and sliced
10 minutes		3 garlic cloves, sliced thinly	
30 minutes			

Heat the oil and butter in a large skillet over a medium heat. Add the onion and cook until soft. Raise the heat to medium–high and add the bell peppers and garlic. Cook for 12–15 minutes, stirring, until the peppers are tender but not mushy. Season with salt and pepper. Remove from the heat.

Cook the pasta in plenty of boiling salted water until al dente. Drain and transfer to a warm serving dish. Add the goat cheese and toss to mix.

Briefly reheat the sauce. Add the basil and olives. Pour over the pasta and toss well to mix. Serve immediately.

tomato sauce
with garlic & basil

		ingredients	
	very easy	5 tbsp extra-virgin olive oil	1 lb/450 g dried spaghetti
		1 onion, chopped finely	large handful fresh basil leaves,
	serves 4	1 lb 12 oz/800 g canned	shredded
		chopped tomatoes	
		4 garlic cloves, cut into fourths	freshly grated Parmesan, to serve
	10 minutes	salt and pepper	
	30 minutes		

Heat the oil in a large pan over a medium heat. Add the onion and cook gently for 5 minutes, until soft. Add the tomatoes and garlic. Bring to a boil, then simmer over a medium–low heat for 25–30 minutes, or until the oil separates from the tomato. Season with salt and pepper.

Cook the pasta in plenty of boiling salted water until al dente. Drain and transfer to a warm serving dish.

Pour the sauce over the pasta. Add the basil and toss well to mix. Serve with Parmesan.

raw tomato sauce with
olive oil, garlic & basil

		ingredients	
extremely easy		1 lb 4 oz/550 g large, ripe tomatoes, peeled, seeded, and diced	3 tbsp chopped fresh oregano or marjoram
serves 4		½ cup extra-virgin olive oil	salt and pepper
		4 garlic cloves, chopped very finely	4 cups dried conchiglie
10 minutes + 30 minutes' standing time		large handful fresh basil leaves, shredded	
8–10 minutes			

Combine the tomatoes, olive oil, garlic, basil, and oregano in a bowl that is large enough to eventually accommodate the cooked pasta. Season generously with salt and pepper. Cover the bowl with plastic wrap and let stand at room temperature for at least 30 minutes.

Cook the pasta in plenty of boiling salted water until al dente. Drain thoroughly and immediately add to the tomatoes.

Toss well to mix. Serve at room temperature.

cherry tomato sauce
with olives

		ingredients	
very easy		4 tbsp olive oil	20–25 black olives, pitted and sliced
		2 lb/900 g cherry tomatoes	pepper
serves 4		2 garlic cloves, chopped very finely	3 cups dried conchiglie
		1 tbsp chopped fresh oregano	zest of ½ lemon, grated
		or marjoram	scant ¼ cup freshly grated Parmesan
10 minutes		¼ tsp dried chili flakes	
30 minutes			

Heat the oil in a large skillet over a medium–high heat.
Add the cherry tomatoes and stir until evenly coated with oil.
Cover and cook for 10–12 minutes, shaking the skillet and stirring
once, until all the tomatoes have split.

Add the garlic, oregano, chili flakes, and olives. Season with
pepper. Reduce the heat to low and simmer, uncovered, for
another 7–10 minutes.

Cook the pasta in plenty of boiling salted water until al dente.
Drain well and transfer to a warm serving dish.

Pour half the sauce over the pasta. Toss well to mix. Spoon the
rest of the sauce over the top. Sprinkle with the grated lemon
zest and Parmesan and serve at once.

roasted red bell pepper sauce

very easy	
serves 4	
10 minutes	
35 minutes	

ingredients

4 red bell peppers, halved and seeded
5 tbsp olive oil
1 small red onion, sliced finely
2 garlic cloves, chopped very finely
2 tbsp chopped fresh
  flatleaf parsley
1 tsp chopped fresh thyme

salt and pepper
3 cups dried penne or rigatoni

TO SERVE
4 tbsp toasted fresh bread crumbs
freshly grated Parmesan

Place the bell peppers cut side down in a roasting pan. Roast in a preheated oven at 425°F/220°C for 15–20 minutes, or until the skin begins to blacken. Let cool slightly. Remove the skin from the bell peppers. Slice the flesh into thin strips.

Heat the oil in a large skillet over a medium heat. Add the onion and cook for 5 minutes, or until soft. Add the garlic and cook until just beginning to color. Stir in the roasted bell pepper strips, parsley, and thyme. Season with salt and pepper. Stir until heated through.

Cook the pasta in plenty of boiling salted water until al dente. Drain well and transfer to a warm serving dish.

Pour the sauce over the pasta and toss well to mix. Sprinkle with the bread crumbs and serve with Parmesan.

roasted garlic
& red bell pepper sauce

		ingredients	
	very easy	6 large garlic cloves, unpeeled	1 tsp chopped fresh thyme or oregano
		14 oz/400 g bottled roasted red bell	salt and pepper
	serves 4	peppers, drained and sliced	12 oz/350 g dried spaghetti, bucatini
		7 oz/200 g canned chopped tomatoes	or linguine
		3 tbsp olive oil	
	10 minutes	¼ tsp dried chili flakes	freshly grated Parmesan, to serve
	30 minutes		

Place the unpeeled garlic cloves in a shallow, ovenproof dish. Roast in a preheated oven at 400°F/200°C for 7–10 minutes, or until the cloves feel soft.

Put the bell peppers, tomatoes, and oil in a food processor or blender, then purée. Squeeze the garlic flesh into the purée. Add the chili flakes and oregano. Season with salt and pepper. Blend again, then scrape into a pan and set aside.

Cook the pasta in plenty of boiling salted water until al dente. Drain and transfer to a warm serving dish.

Reheat the sauce and pour over the pasta. Toss well to mix. Serve at once with Parmesan.

marinated artichoke sauce with onions & tomatoes

		ingredients	
	very easy	10 oz/280 g marinated artichoke hearts (in jar)	14 oz/400 g canned chopped tomatoes
	serves 4	3 tbsp olive oil 1 onion, chopped finely 3 garlic cloves, chopped very finely	salt and pepper 3 cups dried conchiglie scant ¼ cup freshly grated Parmesan
	10 minutes	1 tsp dried oregano ¼ tsp dried chili flakes	3 tbsp chopped fresh flatleaf parsley
	50 minutes		

Drain the artichoke hearts, reserving the marinade. Heat the oil in a large pan over a medium heat. Add the onion and cook for 5 minutes, or until translucent. Add the garlic, oregano, chili flakes, and the reserved marinade. Cook for 5 more minutes.

Stir in the tomatoes. Bring to a boil, then simmer over a medium–low heat for 30 minutes. Season generously with salt and pepper.

Cook the pasta in plenty of boiling salted water until al dente. Drain and transfer to a warm serving dish.

Add the artichokes, Parmesan, and parsley to the sauce. Cook for a few minutes until heated through.

Pour the sauce over the pasta. Toss well to mix. Serve at once.

asparagus & gorgonzola
sauce with cream

		ingredients
	extremely easy	1 lb/450 g asparagus tips olive oil
	serves 4	salt and pepper 8 oz/225 g Gorgonzola, crumbled ¾ cup heavy cream
	10 minutes	3 cups dried penne
	20 minutes	

Place the asparagus tips in a single layer in a shallow ovenproof dish. Sprinkle with a little olive oil. Season with salt and pepper. Turn to coat in the oil and seasoning.

Roast in a preheated oven at 450°F/230°C for 10–12 minutes, or until slightly browned and just tender. Set aside and keep warm.

Combine the crumbled cheese with the cream in a bowl. Season with salt and pepper.

Cook the pasta in plenty of boiling salted water until al dente. Drain and transfer to a warm serving dish.

Immediately add the asparagus and the cheese mixture. Toss well until the cheese has melted and the pasta is coated with the sauce. Serve at once.

spaghetti with
garlic & oil sauce

		ingredients
extremely easy		1 lb/450 g dried spaghetti
		salt
serves 4		½ cup extra-virgin olive oil
		4 garlic cloves, chopped very finely
		¼ tsp dried chili flakes
10 minutes		3 tbsp chopped fresh flatleaf parsley
25 minutes		

Cook the pasta in plenty of boiling salted water until al dente. Drain and transfer to a warm serving dish. Season with salt to taste and keep the dish warm.

Heat the oil in a small pan over a medium–low heat. Add the garlic and chili flakes. Cook for 1–2 minutes, or until the garlic is just beginning to color. Immediately pour the contents of the pan over the pasta. Toss thoroughly to mix.

Sprinkle with the parsley and toss again. Serve immediately.

roasted garlic cream sauce

		ingredients
easy		2 large heads garlic
		2½ cups heavy cream
		3 thin strips lemon peel
serves 4		salt and pepper
		3 cups dried fettuccine
		or tagliatelle
10 minutes		⅓ cup freshly grated Parmesan
		2 tbsp chopped fresh
20 minutes		flatleaf parsley, to serve

Separate the garlic cloves, removing as much of the papery skin as possible, but leaving a thin layer intact. Place the cloves in a shallow ovenproof dish. Roast in a preheated oven at 400°F/200°C for 7–10 minutes until the cloves feel soft.

When the garlic is cool enough to handle, remove the skin. Put the cloves in a small pan with the cream and lemon peel. Bring to a boil, then simmer gently over a low heat for about 5 minutes, or until thickened. Push the sauce through a fine-meshed strainer, pressing with the back of a wooden spoon. Return to the pan. Season with salt and pepper and set aside.

Cook the pasta in plenty of boiling salted water until al dente. Drain and transfer to a warm serving dish. Stir the Parmesan into the sauce and reheat gently. Pour the sauce over the pasta and toss well to mix. Sprinkle with the parsley. Serve immediately.

mushroom & spinach
sauce with feta

very easy	
serves 4	
15 minutes	
20 minutes	

ingredients

3 tbsp olive oil
4 cups mushrooms, sliced
2 garlic cloves, chopped very finely
2 tbsp chopped fresh
  flatleaf parsley
salt and pepper

4 cups dried rigatoni
3 cups trimmed baby spinach,
  chopped coarsely
1 cup hot chicken bouillon
2 oz/55 g feta cheese, crumbled
1 tsp chopped fresh thyme

Heat the oil in a large skillet over a medium–high heat. Add the mushrooms and cook for 5 minutes, or until the moisture starts to evaporate. Add the garlic and parsley, then cook for a few seconds more. Season with salt and pepper. Remove the cooking pan from the heat.

Cook the pasta in plenty of boiling salted water until al dente. Drain and immediately return to the pan.

Add the spinach, hot bouillon and the mushrooms to the pasta. Toss well until the spinach has wilted. Transfer to a warm serving dish. Sprinkle with the feta and thyme and serve at once.

zucchini sauce
with lemon & rosemary

		ingredients	
very easy		6 tbsp olive oil	1 lb/450 g small zucchini, cut into
		1 small onion, sliced very thinly	1½ x ¼ inch/4 cm x 5 mm strips
serves 4		2 garlic cloves, chopped very finely	finely grated peel of 1 lemon
		2 tbsp chopped fresh rosemary	salt and pepper
		1 tbsp chopped fresh	4 cups fusilli
10 minutes		flatleaf parsley	4 tbsp freshly grated Parmesan
20 minutes			

Heat the olive oil in a large skillet over a medium–low heat. Add the onion and gently cook, stirring occasionally, for about 10 minutes, or until golden.

Raise the heat to medium–high. Add the garlic, rosemary, and parsley. Cook for a few seconds, stirring.

Add the zucchini and lemon peel. Cook for 5–7 minutes, stirring occasionally, until the zucchini are just tender. Season with salt and pepper. Remove from the heat.

Cook the pasta in plenty of boiling salted water until al dente. Drain and transfer to a warm serving dish.

Briefly reheat the zucchini. Pour over the pasta and toss well to mix. Sprinkle with the Parmesan and serve immediately.

fish &
seafood sauces

Fish and seafood are ideal candidates for
pasta sauces, especially if you stock up with
pantry basics such as bottled clams and cans
of tuna and anchovies. These need only the
briefest of cooking times, letting you get a
meal on the table in minutes.

Shrimp are an all-time favorite with pasta
and are very versatile. They can be
combined with tomatoes, garlic, and chile
for a robust Mediterranean sauce, or
sizzled oriental-style with ginger and spices.
Smoked salmon, mussels, and scallops can
form the basis of rich cream or tomato-
based sauces that are ideal for entertaining.

spaghetti with anchovies, olives, capers & tomatoes

		ingredients	
	very easy	6 tbsp olive oil	¼ tsp dried chili flakes
		4 anchovy fillets, chopped	salt and pepper
	serves 4	2 garlic cloves, chopped very finely	12 oz/350 g dried spaghetti
		1 lb 12 oz/800 g canned	10–12 black olives, pitted and sliced
		chopped tomatoes	2 tbsp capers, drained
	10 minutes	1 tsp dried oregano	
	35–40 minutes		

Heat the oil with the anchovies in a large skillet over a low heat. Stir until the anchovies dissolve. Add the garlic and cook for a few seconds, or until just beginning to color. Add the tomatoes, oregano, and chili flakes, then season with salt and pepper. Bring to a boil, then simmer over a medium–low heat for 30 minutes, or until the oil begins to separate from the tomatoes.

Cook the pasta in plenty of boiling salted water until al dente. Drain and transfer to a warm serving dish.

Add the olives and capers to the sauce. Pour over the pasta and toss well to mix. Serve immediately.

clam & tomato sauce

		ingredients	
very easy		14 oz/400 g clams or scallops in brine (in jar)	3 tbsp chopped fresh flatleaf parsley
serves 4		4 tbsp olive oil	½ tsp dried chili flakes
		4 garlic cloves, chopped very finely	salt
10 minutes		1 lb 12 oz/800 g canned chopped tomatoes	4 cups dried riccioli or fusilli
35 minutes			

Drain the clams or scallops, reserving the liquid from the jar.

Heat the oil and garlic in a large pan over a low heat. Cook the garlic for a few seconds, or until just beginning to color. Add the tomatoes, the reserved clam juice, parsley, chili flakes, and a little salt. Bring to a boil, then simmer over a medium–low heat for 30 minutes, or until the oil separates from the tomatoes.

Cook the pasta in plenty of boiling salted water until al dente. Drain and transfer to a warm serving dish.

Add the clams to the sauce, stirring until heated through. Pour the sauce over the pasta. Toss well to mix. Serve immediately.

shrimp sauce with tomatoes, garlic & chile

	very easy	
	serves 4	
	10 minutes	
	35 minutes	

ingredients

4 tbsp olive oil
5 garlic cloves, chopped very finely
14 oz/400 g canned chopped
  tomatoes
1 fresh red chile, seeded and chopped
  very finely

salt and pepper
1 lb/450 g dried linguine or spaghetti
12 oz/350 g raw shelled shrimp

2 tbsp chopped fresh
  flatleaf parsley, to garnish

Heat 2 tablespoons of the oil and the garlic in a pan over a medium–low heat. Cook the garlic until just beginning to color. Add the tomatoes and chili. Bring to a boil, then simmer over a medium–low heat for 30 minutes, or until the oil separates from the tomatoes. Season with salt and pepper.

Cook the pasta in plenty of boiling salted water until al dente. Drain and return to the pan.

Heat the remaining oil in a skillet over a high heat. Add the shrimp and stir-fry for 2 minutes until pink. Add the shrimp to the tomato mixture. Stir in the parsley. Simmer over a low heat until bubbling.

Transfer the pasta to a warm serving dish. Pour the sauce over the pasta. Toss well to mix. Sprinkle over the chopped parsley to garnish and serve immediately.

clam & leek sauce

very easy	
serves 4	
10 minutes	
15 minutes	

ingredients

14 oz/400 g clams in brine (in jar)
3 tbsp olive oil
2 large leeks (white part only),
   sliced lengthwise and cut into thin
   2 inch/5 cm strips
2 garlic cloves, chopped very finely
4 tbsp dry white wine

1 bay leaf
salt and pepper
12 oz/350 g dried spaghetti
   or linguine

3 tbsp chopped fresh
   flatleaf parsley, to garnish

Drain the clams, reserving the liquid from the jar.

Heat the oil in a large skillet over a medium–low heat. Add the leeks and garlic, then cook gently for 3–4 minutes, or until the leeks are tender-crisp. Stir in the wine and cook for 1–2 minutes, or until evaporated. Add the bay leaf, clams, and the reserved liquid. Season with salt and pepper. Simmer for 5 minutes, then remove from the heat.

Cook the pasta in plenty of boiling salted water until al dente. Drain and transfer to a warm serving dish.

Briefly reheat the sauce and pour over the pasta. Add the parsley and toss well to mix. Serve immediately.

shrimp & garlic sauce
with cream

		ingredients	
	very easy	3 tbsp olive oil	12 oz/350 g raw shrimp, shelled,
		3 tbsp butter	cut into ½ inch/1 cm pieces
	serves 4	4 garlic cloves, chopped very finely	½ cup heavy cream
		2 tbsp finely diced red bell pepper	salt and pepper
		2 tbsp tomato paste	
	15 minutes	½ cup dry white wine	3 tbsp chopped fresh
		1 lb/450 g tagliatelle or spaghetti	flat leaf parsley, to garnish
	15 minutes		

Heat the oil and butter in a pan over a medium–low heat. Add the garlic and red bell pepper. Cook for a few seconds, or until the garlic is just beginning to color. Stir in the tomato paste and wine. Cook for 10 minutes, stirring.

Cook the pasta in plenty of boiling salted water until al dente. Drain and return to the pan.

Add the shrimp to the sauce and raise the heat to medium–high. Cook for 2 minutes, stirring, until the shrimp turn pink. Reduce the heat and stir in the cream. Cook for 1 minute, stirring constantly, until thickened. Season with salt and pepper.

Transfer the pasta to a warm serving dish. Pour the sauce over the pasta. Sprinkle with the parsley. Toss well to mix and serve at once.

spicy shrimp sauce
with ginger

		ingredients	
very easy	4 tbsp passata (strained tomatoes)	¼ tsp pepper
	1¼ cups light cream	1 lb/450 g dried flat rice noodles
serves 4	1½ tsp grated fresh ginger	3 tbsp vegetable oil
	¼ tsp cayenne	3 garlic cloves, chopped very finely
	1 tbsp lemon juice	1 lb/450 g raw shrimp, shelled
	1 tsp ground cumin	2 tbsp chopped fresh cilantro
10 minutes	1 tsp salt	
10 minutes		

Combine the passata, cream, ginger, cayenne, lemon juice, cumin, salt, and pepper in a small pan, mixing well. Cook the mixture over a medium heat, stirring, until bubbling, then remove from the heat.

Cook the noodles according to the packet instructions. Drain and transfer to a warm serving dish.

Heat the oil and garlic in a large skillet over a medium–low heat. Cook until the garlic just begins to color. Add the shrimp and raise the heat to medium–high. Stir-fry for 2 minutes, or until the shrimp are pink. Stir in the sauce and 1 tablespoon of the cilantro. Cook for another minute.

Pour the shrimp mixture over the noodles. Sprinkle with the remaining cilantro and serve immediately.

shrimp sauce with lemon & herbs

		ingredients	

	very easy	12 oz/350 g dried spaghettini
		  or vermicelli
			3 tbsp chopped fresh
			  flatleaf parsley

	serves 4	4 tbsp olive oil 4 tbsp butter 8 scallions, green part included,	3 tbsp shredded fresh basil 1 tbsp chopped fresh marjoram or oregano
	15–20 minutes	sliced thinly 1 lb/450 g raw shelled shrimp juice and finely grated peel	2 tsp chopped fresh thyme 1 cup chicken bouillon salt and pepper
	10 minutes	of ½ lemon	

Cook the pasta in plenty of boiling salted water until al dente. Drain and return to the pan and cover to keep warm.

Heat the oil and butter in a large skillet over a medium–high heat. Add the scallions and shrimp. Stir-fry for 2 minutes, or until the shrimp turn pink. Reduce the heat to medium. Stir in the lemon juice and peel, herbs, and chicken bouillon. Season with salt and pepper. Simmer until heated through.

Transfer the pasta to a warm serving dish. Pour the shrimp mixture over the pasta and toss well to mix. Serve immediately.

scallops with porcini & cream sauce

		ingredients	
very easy	1⅓ cups dried porcini mushrooms	1 cup heavy cream
	generous 2 cups hot water	salt and pepper
serves 4	3 tbsp olive oil	12 oz/350 g dried fettuccine
	3 tbsp butter	or pappardelle
	1½ cups scallops, sliced	
10 minutes +20 minutes to soak mushrooms	2 garlic cloves, chopped very finely	2 tbsp chopped fresh
	2 tbsp lemon juice	flatleaf parsley, to serve
25 minutes		

Put the porcini and hot water in a bowl. Let soak for 20 minutes. Strain the mushrooms, reserving the soaking water, and chop coarsely. Line a strainer with paper towels and strain the mushroom water into a bowl.

Heat the oil and butter in a large skillet over a medium heat. Add the scallops and cook for 2 minutes, or until just golden. Add the garlic and mushrooms, then stir-fry for another minute.

Stir in the lemon juice, cream, and ½ cup of the mushroom water. Bring to a boil, then simmer over a medium heat for 2–3 minutes, stirring constantly, until the liquid is reduced by half. Season with salt and pepper. Remove from the heat.

Cook the pasta in plenty of boiling salted water until al dente. Drain and transfer to a warm serving dish. Briefly reheat the sauce and pour over the pasta. Sprinkle with the parsley and toss well to mix. Serve immediately.

tuna with garlic,
lemon, capers & olives

		ingredients	
	extremely easy	3 cups dried conchiglie or gnocchi	2 tbsp lemon juice
		4 tbsp olive oil	1 tbsp capers, drained
	serves 4	4 tbsp butter	10–12 black olives, pitted and sliced
		3 large garlic cloves, sliced thinly	
		7 oz/200 g canned tuna, drained	
	10 minutes	and broken into chunks	2 tbsp chopped fresh
			flatleaf parsley, to serve
	10 minutes		

Cook the pasta in plenty of boiling salted water until al dente. Drain and return to the pan.

Heat the olive oil and half the butter in a skillet over a medium–low heat. Add the garlic and cook for a few seconds, or until just beginning to color. Reduce the heat to low. Add the tuna, lemon juice, capers, and olives. Stir gently until all the ingredients are heated through.

Transfer the pasta to a warm serving dish. Pour the tuna mixture over the pasta. Add the parsley and remaining butter. Toss well to mix. Serve immediately.

mussels with tomatoes, bell peppers & olives

		ingredients	
very easy		12½ cups mussels	¼ tsp dried chili flakes
		1 large onion, chopped finely	salt and pepper
serves 4		1 cup dry white wine	1 lb/450 g riccioli or fettucine
		3 tbsp olive oil	10–12 black olives, pitted and sliced
20 minutes		3 garlic cloves, chopped very finely	
		2 yellow bell peppers, seeded and diced	6 tbsp shredded fresh basil, to serve
20 minutes		14 oz/400 g canned chopped tomatoes	

Clean the mussels by scrubbing the shells and pulling out any beards that are attached. Rinse well and discard any with broken shells and any that do not close when tapped. Put the mussels in a large pan with the onion and white wine. Cover and cook over a medium heat for 3–4 minutes, shaking the pan, until the mussels open. Remove from the heat. Lift out the mussels with a perforated spoon, reserving the liquid. Discard any that remain closed. Remove the rest of the mussels from their shells.

Heat the olive oil and garlic in a skillet over a medium–low heat. Cook until the garlic is just beginning to color. Add the bell peppers, tomatoes, chili flakes and 4 tablespoons of the mussel liquid. Bring to a boil, then simmer over a medium heat for 15 minutes, or until slightly reduced. Season with salt and pepper. Cook the pasta until al dente. Drain and transfer to a serving dish. Add the mussels and olives to the sauce; stir until heated. Pour onto the pasta. Add the basil and mix well. Serve at once.

mussels with white wine, garlic & parsley

		ingredients	
very easy	14 cups mussels	5 tbsp chopped fresh
	1 large onion, chopped	flatleaf parsley
serves 4	3 garlic cloves, chopped	1 tbsp chopped fresh rosemary
	very finely	4 tbsp butter
	generous 2 cups dry white wine	salt and pepper
20 minutes	1 bay leaf	1 lb/450 g dried tagliatelle or other
	2 sprigs of fresh thyme	broad-ribboned pasta
10 minutes		

Clean the mussels by scrubbing the shells and pulling out any beards that are attached. Rinse well, discarding any with broken shells or that remain open when tapped. Put the onion, garlic, white wine, herbs, and 2 tablespoons of the butter in a pan. Bring to a boil, then reduce the heat. Add the mussels. Season to taste. Cover and cook over a medium heat for 3–4 minutes, shaking the pan, until the mussels open. Remove from the heat. Lift out the mussels with a perforated spoon, reserving the liquid. Discard any that remain closed. Remove most of the others from their shells, reserving a few in their shells to garnish.

Cook the pasta until al dente. Drain and put the pasta into bowls. Spoon the mussels over the pasta. Strain the mussel liquid and return to the pan. Add the remaining butter and heat until melted. Pour over the pasta, then garnish with the mussels in their shells and serve immediately.

smoked salmon, sour cream & mustard sauce

		ingredients	
extremely easy	1 lb/450 g tagliatelle or conchiglie	8 oz/225 g smoked salmon, cut into bite-size pieces	
serves 4	1¼ cups sour cream 2 tsp Dijon mustard 4 large scallions, sliced finely	finely grated peel of ½ lemon pepper 2 tbsp chopped fresh chives	
10 minutes			
10 minutes			

Cook the pasta in plenty of boiling salted water until al dente. Drain and return to the pan. Add the sour cream, mustard, scallions, smoked salmon, and lemon peel to the pasta. Stir over a low heat until heated through. Season with pepper.

Transfer to a serving dish. Sprinkle with the chives. Serve warm or at room temperature.

hot cajun seafood sauce

		ingredients	
	very easy	generous 2 cups whipping cream	1 lb/450 g dried fusilli or tagliatelle
		8 scallions, sliced thinly	scant ½ cup freshly grated Gruyère
	serves 4	scant 1 cup fresh flatleaf parsley,	scant ¼ cup freshly grated Parmesan
		chopped	2 tbsp olive oil
		1 tbsp chopped fresh thyme	8 oz/225 g raw shelled shrimp
		½ tbsp freshly ground black pepper	1 cup scallops, sliced
	15 minutes	½–1 tsp dried chili flakes	
		1 tsp salt	1 tbsp shredded fresh basil, to serve
	20 minutes		

Heat the cream in a large pan over a medium heat, stirring constantly. When almost boiling, reduce the heat and add the scallions, parsley, thyme, pepper, chili flakes, and salt. Simmer for 7–8 minutes, stirring, until thickened. Remove from the heat.

Cook the pasta in plenty of boiling salted water until al dente. Drain and return to the pan. Add the cream mixture and the cheeses to the pasta. Toss over a low heat until the cheeses have melted. Transfer to a warm serving dish.

Heat the oil in a large skillet over a medium–high heat. Add the shrimp and scallops. Stir-fry for 2–3 minutes, or until the shrimp have just turned pink.

Pour the seafood over the pasta and toss well to mix. Sprinkle with the basil. Serve immediately.

index